Bear in Sunshine
L'ours au soleil

Stella Blackstone
Debbie Harter

Barefoot Books
Celebrating Art and Story

Bear likes to play
when the sun shines.

L'ours aime jouer
quand le soleil brille.

**Bear likes to sing
in the rain.**

L'ours aime chanter
sous la pluie.

He flies his red kite
when it's windy.

Il fait voler son cerf-volant
rouge quand le vent souffle.

**When it's icy,
he skates in the lane.**

Quand tout est gelé, il patine sur le chemin.

**Bear likes to paint
when it's foggy.**

L'ours aime peindre
quand il y a du brouillard .

When it's stormy, he hides in his bed.

**Quand l'orage éclate,
il se cache dans son lit.**

When it snows, he likes to make snow-bears.

**Quand la neige tombe,
il aime faire des ours de neige.**

When the moon shines
he stands on his head.

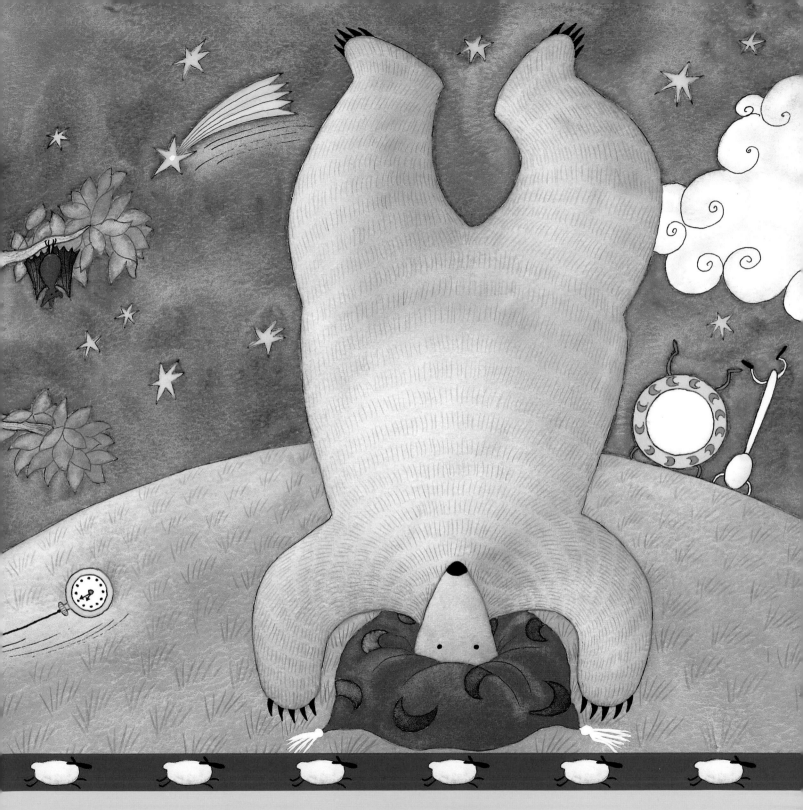

Quand la lune brille,
il se tient sur la tête.

Whatever the weather, snow, rain or sun,

**Quel que soit le temps,
neige, pluie ou soleil,**

Bear always knows
how to have fun!

l'ours trouve toujours
de quoi s'amuser!

Spring
Printemps

Summer
Été

Autumn
Automne

Winter
Hiver

Vocabulary / Vocabulaire

weather – temps

sun – soleil

moon – lune

rain – pluie

kite – cerf-volant

wind – vent

ice – glace

fog – brouillard

storm – orage

snow – neige

Barefoot Books
124 Walcot Street
Bath BA1 5BG

Barefoot Books
2067 Massachusetts Ave
Cambridge, MA 02140

Text copyright © 2001 by Stella Blackstone Illustrations copyright © 2001 by Debbie Harter
Translation by Servane Champion

The moral rights of Stella Blackstone and Debbie Harter have been asserted.

First published in Great Britain by Barefoot Books Ltd and in the United States of America
by Barefoot Books Inc in 2001. This edition published in 2009

This book has been printed in China by Printplus Ltd on 100% acid-free paper

ISBN 978-1-84686-388-2

1 3 5 7 9 8 6 4 2

British Cataloguing-in-Publication Data:
a catalogue record for this book is available from the British Library

Library of Congress Cataloging-in-Publication Data available under LCCN 2009003088